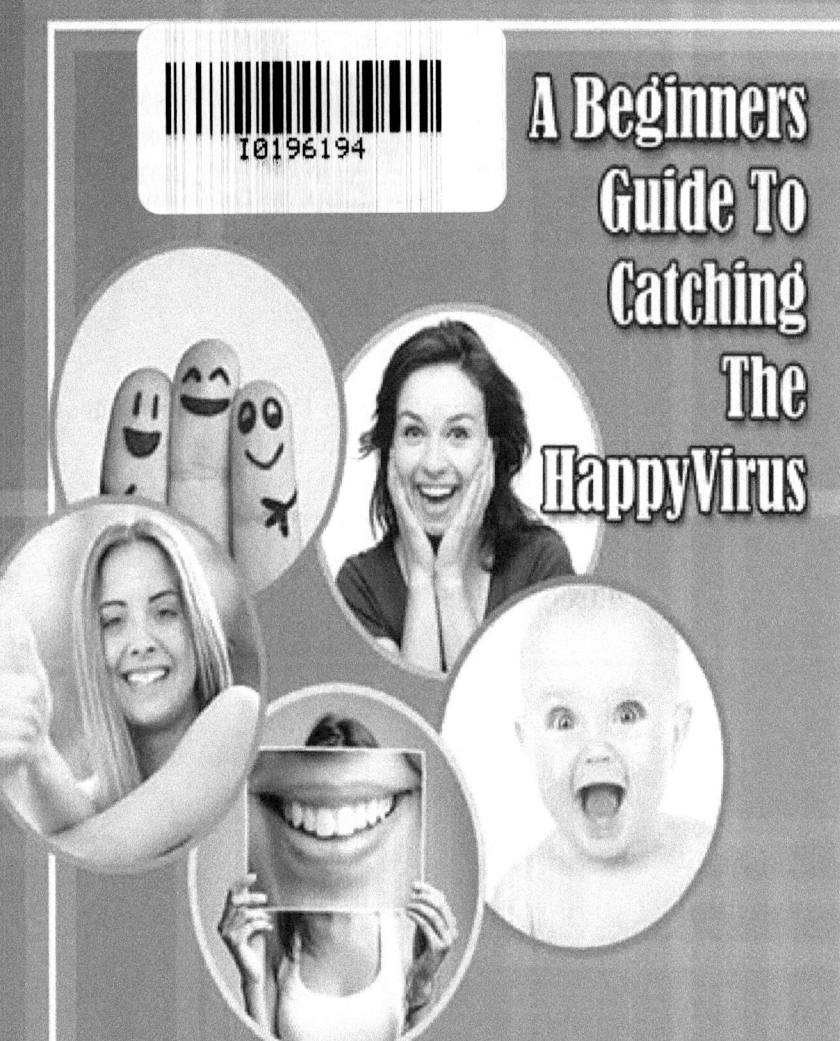

© 2013 James Monty

All Rights Reserved

Founder Thoughts in Pen

For more information about James Monty's writings about personal growth, visit www.thoughtsinpen.com

Other works by James include his first book, *How To Enjoy Eating With Diabetes* and many free eBooks on self-discovery available on his web site.

Creative Writing Creative Solutions

This Book Is Dedicated To:

William "Billy" Joyce

A person of profound happiness and smiles; a nephew, a son, and a friend. Billy lived with me and my wife Mary for the final ten years of his life. His life was cut short on July 10th, 2009 at only 19 years young. The ideal of friendship was Billy's compass in life, and his legacy in death. Never have I met a person of any age having a more profound or positive effect on his world. Never have I met a person with such inner peace, and joy fulfilled through the smiles and happiness he brought others. Thank you for teaching me.

> "Happiness is like a butterfly which, when pursued, is always beyond our grasp, but, if you will sit down quietly, may alight upon you." _Nathaniel Hawthorne

Contents

Preface 5

Introduction 9

What Is Our Belief System? 17

How Do Belief Systems Work? 19

How Do I Recognize Beliefs? 21

Changing Unwanted Beliefs 23

Rewiring 26

What Is Happiness? 35

Why Does That Make Me Feel Unhappy? 40

What Is Forgiveness? 46

How Our Beliefs Affect Forgiveness 49

Forgiving Others 61

Forgiving Ourselves 66

The Negative People In Our Life 70

Holding On To The Negative 73

Being Your Own Worst Enemy 77

Oh! The Drama...81

Self-Esteem...84

Does Self-Esteem Really Exist?.......................................90

When Does Self-Esteem Begin?.....................................93

Self-Worth...96

Positive Thinking?...100

How Does It Affect Me?..103

What Can I Do About It?...107

Our Right To Be Happy...110

Is Change Really That Easy?..112

Identifying Change Needed..117

Bringing About Change...121

Lasting Change...126

The Joy Within..131

Preface

I want to introduce you to the HappyVirus. It is a strain of virus that has already infected millions of people in the United States alone. It has survived the toughest of times like poverty, war and illness. The only known killer of the HappyVirus is having an attitude of fear, mistrust, or anger hidden inside the human brain. The effects of not being infected are sadness, uncertainty, an inability to smile and the loss of good times in your life. While some people have deep-rooted challenges that give them the appearance of being immune to the HappyVirus, the majority of those uninfected have the ability within themselves to embrace the virus and let it run rampart.

I have found through my 60 years of living that even I have times when the HappyVirus goes into remission. I have also found that I have the power to bring it to the forefront whenever I choose to, sometimes easily and other times with a bit more of a challenge.

I have always been what you would call a people person, someone who finds good in all people and refuses to waste time being unhappy. I would say that I have been infected by the HappyVirus since I was a child, but it really became apparent when I began my career in sales at about 30 years old. I have found that there is an indefinable sense of satisfaction and joy in helping others get past their challenges, and spreading the HappyVirus to everyone I come in contact with. Although, in all honesty, there have been times when people have asked me if I have something wrong with me because I am happy so much.

Don't get me wrong, I get angry, sad and deflated at times, just like all normal human beings, but I rebound fast, very fast. A HappyVirus infection is the only way to live. Watch the smiles and laughter it causes; you will be so amazed.

So let me start my story of the HappyVirus and how you can catch it for all its glory. Thank you for purchasing my book. I hope it brings you much happiness, you deserve it.

Here 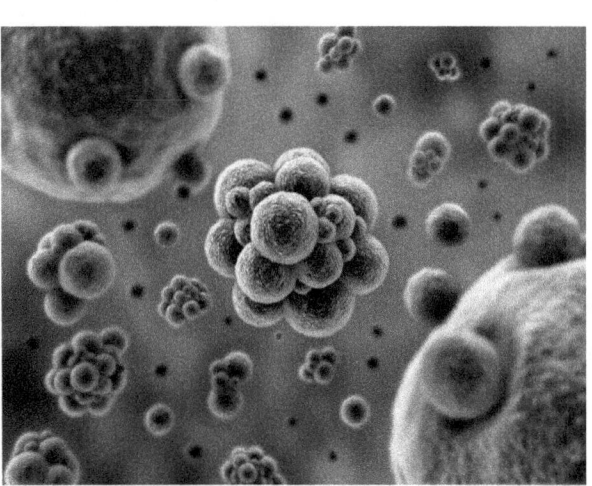 is a picture of the HappyVirus through a microscope.

As you can see, it doesn't really look any different than a regular virus or germ, but if we use an electron microscope to get a closer, more detailed look, you can see the difference. Its shape and color are very distinctive.

It is a friendly and happy virus. If we could take a movie of it, you would see it dancing and making those undeniable sounds of laughter.

So let's begin our journey on how to unleash the HappyVirus in you.

Introduction

I remember when I met the Dalai Lama, back on May 10, 1998 at Brandeis University. I was managing a sign company which did all the signage for his arrival, and I was given three tickets to see him.

I went with my psychology teacher, Charlene, and her husband. We got to sit in the second row, right on the aisle. The most delightful surprise was when the Dalai Lama took a break from talking, and he invited the first two rows to join him in the back for some tea.

I never thought meeting him could have such a profound effect on me. It is difficult to describe, but there was a mystique about his manner and voice that commanded, in a compassionate way, that you listen and watch or you will have denied yourself a moment of warmth and hope that no other could give. I went to the back and sat down, but before he sat down, he came by each person and asked each individual why they were there and what they did for work.

> "The secret of health for both mind and body is not to mourn for the past, worry about the future, or anticipate troubles, but to live in the present moment wisely and earnestly."- Buddha

When I told him I had done all the signage, including that large emblem for Brandeis University, he announced to the rest of the table, "This young man is responsible for the wonderful signs and posters we've all got to enjoy during our visit here." He followed that statement with a pat on my shoulder and one of his chuckles that seem to go inside you and extract a smile.

As I said, Charlene was one of my psychology professors at University of Massachusetts, Lowell. I asked her to come with me because I had five classes with her at the time, and in her teaching, she always had a tendency to sprinkle in the Eastern cultures and the effect they were having on Western psychology. Her manner and style got me so excited about psychology that I changed my major from Business Administration to Psychology, and have absolutely loved every minute of my education. Wow, that might have been the first time I was infected with the HappyVirus.

It made for some very interesting classes and certainly broadened my perspective on the different ways cultures influence people. While Western cultures tend to externalize their spirituality, Eastern cultures internalize it.

"In the sky, there is no distinction of east and west; people create distinctions out of their own minds and then believe them to be true." -Buddha

It is important to remember that we not talking about religion. Buddhists do not worship a God, although they do believe in the existence of one. Rather, Buddhism is structured in such a way that some of the things people of other religions pray to a God for, Buddhists look within themselves to accomplish.

An example of this would be when Christians would pray to Jesus for forgiveness for something they have done wrong. Instead, Buddhists internalize that and find it within themselves to find the forgiveness for a wrong done to them, or something they have done to another. Buddhism can be a demanding philosophy, since it places the onus on the individual to fix the problems they have in life, especially in the western cultures where we look to God for guidance. If a Buddhist wishes to improve the level of happiness in their life, they must search within themselves to find the means to accomplish this. We in American culture have gotten away from that philosophy. We have begun to evolve into people that look outside themselves for justification of our own actions, as well as for approval for something we have done. We have confused happiness with pleasure.

The difference between happiness and pleasure is that pleasure is a temporary and often short lived, state of mind. It is usually brought on by external forces. Happiness can also be brought on by external forces, but it is maintained by our inner self.

This book is about relearning how to deal with the fact that the hand life deals us is from our own deck of cards. Nobody should have the right to determine when we feel good about ourselves. Nobody should have the right to be able to decide when we will or will not be happy.

> "You yourself, as much as anyone in the entire universe, deserve your love and affection." -Buddha

These are our choices, and completely under our control. I will provide information and ways to help you not only see and understand this, but also help you put a plan into action that will ensure you arrive at a place of happiness; in complete control of the self.

The word "happy" is derived from the noun "HAP," meaning chance or good fortune. It is important to remember that happiness is much more than a state of feeling good or hopeful. Any of us can feel good without being happy.

When we have a problem, we may go out to have a few drinks to "drown our sorrows". The alcohol may make us feel good, but we are far from happy. Some people will light up a joint of marijuana to make themselves feel good, but you can rest assured they do not get happiness in the true sense of the word from this activity.

Our *quest* for happiness will even sometimes cause us to do things that provide only a fleeting moment of happiness. Later, we feel a regret for our actions that is far stronger than the perceived happiness we had hoped to gain.

Searching for happiness is a quest with no end. When we struggle to find happiness, we lose sight of what happiness really is, and we are most likely passing by much happiness in our misguided journey.

"Happiness comes when you believe in what you are doing, know what you are doing, and love what you are doing." - Brian Tracy

We cannot seek happiness as if it were a prize for our taking. Our happiness depends on the inner self. Far too many think happiness is to be given to them from others, or found through their deeds and accomplishments.

The happiness that is in our heart and soul is a lasting happiness. It is not dependent on any outside source for replenishment. Each of us has the capacity to bring happiness to others through our friendship, love, and caring.

Think about when you do something to make another smile. It may be something as simple as getting a baby to smile through your silliness, or it may be something deeper like helping a friend through a tough time. Don't you feel a warmth and state of satisfaction inside that is unlike any other?

Happiness in dependent on our own actions. Yes, we can get temporary feelings of happiness from external events. If you scratch a winning lottery ticket, you feel a quick burst of elation at winning, but it is short lived and fades quickly.

It is most important to remember that happiness is not a goal. It is the path we take in life that leads to the ultimate goal of fulfillment and enlightenment.

If you make happiness a goal you are working toward, rather than a journey of many happy events, you will miss so much happiness along the way. This will cause you to think it to be unattainable in your life, and find yourself settling for less in your life than you deserve.

The Happyvirus is the most fun and enlightening virus you will ever encounter. Unlike other viruses, the Happyvirus is most often spread with a smile or a laugh. It is the most contagious of all viruses. You will be amazed at both how quickly you can pass it along to others, and how easily they can pass it on to others.

What Is Our Belief System?

Our belief systems are things we were taught or exposed to while growing up. Some were physically taught to us, while some we simply picked up through the actions and body language of others.

It is important to remember that our beliefs drive our behavior and are often not based on proof or experience. Most people never question the validity of their beliefs, and go through life treating them as if they had undisputed proof that the beliefs are valid and true to form. Of course, nothing could be further from the truth. After all, the word belief literally means a feeling of being sure that someone or something exists, or that something is true; the key word there is "feeling".

> "Whatever you do, you must remain nimble in your thinking. Do not become so attached to any one belief that you cannot see past it to another possibility." -Christopher Paolini

I guess the ultimate example of a belief is with God, whichever form she may take in your religious culture. As of this writing, there are approximately 7.023 billion people on our dear planet. And, according to answers.com, as of 2005,

86% of those people believe in a God. In the United States that number is actually 95%. Well, enough stats and more reasoning.

Our life is full of beliefs that we act on every day and never question. These are the values that are taught to us as children and have been passed down through generations. As we are growing and learning, these values are essential to having a strong family foundation. They build trust and confidence between family members, while allowing us to have the comfort and confidence in knowing family is there for us when needed. Without going into details (that's a book to come) about each one, here are some of those values typical to most families.

1. Forgiveness
2. Traditions
3. Responsibility
4. Respect
5. Trust
6. Love
7. Compassion

How Do Belief Systems Work?

I am going to use our nervous system as an analogy for how our belief system works for us.

You see, we actually have two nervous systems; the Somatic and the Autonomic. The Somatic is the part that is associated with the voluntary control of our body: walking, chewing, eye movement. The autonomic system does the behind the scenes work without us having to think about it: breathing, heartbeat, and all the functions our organs do every minute of every day.

Can you imagine what it would be like if we had to think about everything our body is doing at any given moment in time? I think we would go bonkers. So now you have a complete look at neurology according to Jim. Don't you feel smart?

> "It's what you choose to believe that makes you the person you are."
>
> -Karen Marie Moning

Our belief system operates the same as our Autonomic nervous system; functioning in the background, while consciously we remain oblivious to the power and influence it has over our actions and behavior. We respond automatically, much like a television does to the remote.

Of course some of these reactions are protective in nature. They keep us from hurting ourselves by alerting us to dangers before we get in harm's way. However, most are simply ideals and beliefs that have been passed down through generations.

I am sure you can recall hearing your parents or even yourself say, "This is how my mother did it and the generations before her", or "Your grandfather taught me this when I was your age and if it was good enough for him, it's good enough for me." And as a result, we truly believe, "So it is written and so it shall be."

How Do I Recognize Beliefs?

If we are to bring change into our lives for the better, we need to give conscious thought to some of these beliefs. We should also question their validity by determining if there is any fact to them. We need to stop taking for granted that the beliefs are true and must be lived by.

If we continue to accept them as fact, and with the attitude of, "This is how it has always been and always will be", then you can bet that is exactly the way things will remain. We have to sit down and take the time to think about the beliefs we have. Identifying them requires looking at ourselves honestly and openly, so we can discover the "ways" we do things and react to things. Then we can determine if that is the way we really want to be, or has this been taught to us.

"Belief was immune to logic; it operated by its own laws." - James Siegel

If we continue to do the same things in our lives, we can't expect anything to change; that is insanity. And of course it is much safer and convenient for us to accept these beliefs as the law, so we can avoid the confrontation that challenging them will bring.

There is always the fear of change. It is our innate fear of the unknown and the fear of uncertainty that change brings into our lives. Certainty is necessary for us to function and feel safe in our everyday lives. Certainty is the knowledge that we are free of doubt in the actions we are undertaking.

The simple action of getting into your car in the morning and driving to work is certainty in action. You have driven it many times and know the road to take. But, put a detour in the usual route and now you have some doubt about driving to work. Hence, certainty no longer exists. You know the feeling because you experience it anytime something in your daily routine is changed.

Our beliefs provide us with the certainty we need while we are growing up. This sense of certainty is essential. It provides the safety and security necessary for us to be able to go out and make friends or feel love, and for us to trust other people.

Changing Unwanted Beliefs

I will give a brief description here which I will elaborate on later in this book. The most important thing to remember about our beliefs is that they were someone else's beliefs passed to us when we were looking for the experienced older person to help guide us. In most cases, we were too young and naive to question the validity of those beliefs and thus allowed years of embedding them into our thinking, until we simply and blindly accept them as the truth.

Some of these beliefs are silly and superstitious, well to me anyway. A black cat means bad luck; breaking a mirror is 7 years bad luck (I always wondered if the size of the mirror mattered) and of course, walking under a ladder. I think the ladder one came about after a few clumsy people bumped the ladder and it fell.

"But once you have a belief system everything that comes in either gets ignored if it doesn't fit the belief system or gets distorted enough so that it can fit into the belief system. You gotta be continually revising your map of the world." — Robert Anton Wilson

When was the last time you cracked the wishbone in a chicken for good luck? Anyway, think of how long these superstitions have endured. Now, apply this to yourself growing up. Most likely you were taught these and many others, but you were also taught some beliefs that are specific to your family.

Do you remember, "Spare the rod, Spoil the child?" This was the way of my home as I grew up. Of course then in the olden days, it was more prevalent than today. But never the less, it was taught to me through my growing years, and I can remember always saying to myself that I would never run my house like that.

But, then as my children were growing up we experienced the normal growing pains with them. I can recall saying on a few occasions, "Hey, it worked for my Dad, it'll work for me.", mostly in frustration of course. My point is that I hadn't thought about that belief for over 15 years, but when the situation arose in my life, it popped right out and there it was.

Take a moment to seriously think about some things you were taught that you have, since becoming an adult, changed in your life because they couldn't stand the test of time. How many of these do you have inside you that you carry around every day, without giving them a single thought?

> "Deciding what you want to do with your life is half the battle. The other half is deciding who you are doing it for."
> -James Monty

My bet is that if you sit and write them down, you will be more than a bit surprised by the answer. This is what you need to do in order to identify them, so you can determine which ones are not who you are today. The next time you do something and shortly thereafter question yourself about why you did it, pause and think. It may be a belief rearing its ugly head,

Rewiring

The premise of Buddhism to retrain the mind to find the causes of our suffering, and to replace them with new thoughts of happiness. This is basically the premise of cognitive therapy as well. We locate the cause of our pain and change our thoughts' patterns to re-frame it, so we can get by it and alter the effect it has on our happiness.

Western psychology differs in that its goal is not re-framing, but rather identifying and circumventing the effect a negative thought or happening has on our direction. The roads taken differ, but the destination is the same - happiness and joy in our lives.

Life is not about making others happy. Life is about sharing your happiness with others.

We must remember where we are as humans in terms of evolution. The changes brought on through evolution are usually slow to the tune of tens of thousands or even millions of years. In the case of the human brain, we have put it in a position where we are asking it to adapt to massive amounts of change in only a few thousand years.

History tells us that Columbus discovered America in 1492. This is 2013. Just for a minute, think about the changes America and the world has been through in only 521 years.

As a result of the quickened evolution of the human brain, some of the instinctual behaviors programmed in us are no longer used in the same way. For example, our fight or flight response is there to identify danger and give us the necessary adrenalin and survival instincts to know if we should fight or run away. It basically supplied everything we needed to give us the best chance of surviving an incident.

Today, we no longer have to worry about confronting a dinosaur, and for the most part, we rarely have a life threatening event to be concerned about. We still have the fight or flight instincts within us, but now they are triggered by more mundane occurrences.

> "If finding your happiness depends on another, you are destined to live unsatisfied." James Monty

For example, someone may have a fear of going into an elevator with people in it. As a result, it triggers the fight or flight response which causes adrenalin to flow more, and they begin to sweat and get very tense. Not understanding that the over-reaction is wired in us, one starts to have negative thoughts about one's self, as though we were a weak or even defective person since no one else is experiencing what we are. This snowballs until we begin to ask ourselves, "What is wrong with me?" So, what is there to protect us has now been labelled, by our own mind, as a flaw in our character.

Medical technology has advanced at such an unprecedented rate that now, with the use of an MRI, they can pinpoint any area of our body for a closer look at exactly what is going on. This is especially significant with the brain. It has given a new, clearer meaning to the term "rewiring." The ability to grow new neural connections has gone from theoretical to proven. Research done at the National Institutes of Mental Health, by Doctors Avi Karni and Leslie Underleider, had participants perform a simple finger tapping exercise. Using an MRI scan, they identified the parts of the brain involved in the task.

The subjects were then instructed to perform the same finger tapping exercise for 4 weeks, so that they became faster and more proficient. At the end of the 4 weeks, the participants were given another MRI scan while finger tapping. This showed that the area of the brain involved in the task had expanded.

This meant that the brain had recruited new neural connections apart from those that had originally been involved in performing the task; it had rewired itself.

> "Stop holding onto what has past. Stop reaching for what has yet to come. Grab hold of all that is good now." - James Monty

The importance of this study, and many others that found the same results, is that rewiring of the brain has been taken from theoretical to practical. Now there is concrete evidence that we can change our brain to replace and enhance the areas we need to "fix". It has taken the brain from the realm of possibility to actuality.

This is powerful information to have when we are trying to overcome a fear or change an aspect of our personality we are unhappy with. It is no longer a case of "we may be able to do it".

It is now a fact that every human being has within themselves that ability to reprogram their brain to enhance their life. I am not a psychologist, but this seems as though it could have huge implications in cognitive therapy.

Do you remember when you were going to ride your bicycle for the first time without the training wheels? You watched as your parent took off the wheels thinking about how scary it was going to be. Your parents said you could do it, but you weren't sure and remained scared.

Well, you did ride your bike without the training wheels. And as time went on, a very short time, you would come out of the house and jump on your bike and ride away. Then riding it was a natural feeling requiring very little, if any, thought.

That is your brain being rewired. It set itself so you would have a better sense of balance, more confidence, and eventually brought you to the point of not having to think about riding your bike. It just happened.

Think of how many times in your life this has happened to you. Some other examples of this great change are common events that most people share: ice skating, roller skating, skate boarding, and learning to drive. These all become second nature to us over time, and are now as natural to us as breathing.

The Rite To Happiness

I have read many books on happiness in my personal quest to improve my mindset and be happier. Of all the writings, whether scientific or motivational, I found the most direct and applicable style to be the writings of the Dali Lama and Buddhism.

The beauty of Buddhism is that there is no requirement to adhere to a new religion, or change the way you currently approach religion. It is based on the inner self and most definitely encourages a person to engage in religious activities.

"Happiness is the art of never holding in your mind the memory of any unpleasant thing that has passed." -Unknown

Those of us in the Western cultures, such as the United States, have a generalized view of the world; it is a good place and we are entitled to a good life based on our experiences here. We don't see the suffering in other parts of the world, like the Eastern countries. Sure, we see news clips of fighting and terrorism in some parts, but we don't see the plight of peoples in the poorest countries. We are shielded from the hunger, poverty and disease these people live with every day.

As such, we have a view through rose-colored glasses that the world is basically a good place to live and that we are good people and deserve to have good things. We take for granted the good things we have in our lives and have adopted a feeling of being due happiness. These outside factors have become the determinant in how happy we will be.

This has caused misdirection in our pursuit of happiness. Even that term, "pursuit of happiness", as in the Constitution of the United States, is a misnomer. If happiness is to be a part of your life, it is not attainable through pursuit. The word pursue itself means to try to catch or capture something for a long period of time. So to pursue happiness would mean that we have made it a goal in life and as mentioned earlier, it is not a goal. It is an internal state of being that is in all of us as I write this. Our challenge is to look at ourselves for our happiness and not at outside sources and not to tell our self, "I will be happy when this or that happens."

"It isn't what you have, or who you are, or where you are, or what you are doing that makes you happy or unhappy. It is what you think about." -Dale Carnegie

We all know that if we are to have a prosperous life, then we have to be smart and work for that goal. We know prosperity will not be given to us by anyone. Yet, we so often look to others for our happiness. We seek approval from our friends and family. We look to our boss at work to give us that proverbial pat on the back to bring us happiness at work.

I guess the simplest way to put it is that we have lost our way. We have forgotten the simple truth that our long term happiness in life is of our own accord. Yes, we do have a right to be happy, but the rite of happiness is of our own making.

What Is Happiness?

The definition of happiness is as varied as the people living on our planet. We each have established our versions of what happiness is as well as how happiness feels. As such, we also have our own expectations of how happiness can be achieved.

Unfortunately, too many still largely depend on external factors for happiness. Their happiness is not based on internal satisfaction in their own life, but on the approval of others. Or, it is based on the material gains achieved. This has become something we are taught from the time we are born. Psychologists define it as "subjective well-being". It is a combination of our level of satisfaction with our life and the presence of more positive than negative thoughts or emotions. This definition almost seems a tad over simplified if you consider the power of any given emotion.

> "If you are worried about what is going to happen tomorrow, whether it happens or not, you have needlessly suffered" -James Monty

A positive-thought-based person can have an overpowering negative event overshadow any and all positive feelings they may have at any given time. This does not make that person a negative person per say. So, we need a less generalized definition to better understand a happy person. Since happiness is subjective in its nature and each of us seeks our own version of happiness, how can each of us reach the same goal if we differ in exactly what that goal is? We can start with one solid premise.

All of us are born with the ability to attain a state of happiness in our lives. From the simplistic happiness an infant gets from receiving milk from its mother, to the happiness a toddler feels when given a smile of approval from a parent, happiness is within the mind of each. It is not a learned behavior or feeling. What determines the path of definitive happiness in each of us is the lessons learned as we grow older.

We begin to define our happiness in terms of what actions bring approval from our parents. So, this inert ability is being brought out in us by external forces, and not what we feel inside of our own accord.

It must be taught this way since at that young age we could not possibly hope to understand the true meaning of happiness. We are not being taught what happiness is, but rather how to initiate the feeling of being happy.

At this stage of our life, we are developing our anchors that trigger our happiness response. These anchors will be with us for our entire life in one form or another. Some will be replaced as we begin to become more independent in our thinking, and some will remain with us as beliefs we were taught. Some of these we have never reevaluated or brought into question.

The ones that remain as beliefs are the potentially dangerous ones, because in many cases they hide in our subconscious. They randomly rear their ugly heads, in most cases without us even being aware that they are controlling our response at that given moment. We unwillingly subject ourselves to the consequences they may bring, never realizing that it is a learned belief that is controlling our response. If you remember from earlier in this book, our belief systems can make us unwitting subjects of their power. That is why it is so important and vital that, through self-examination, we identify and change those that do not reflect our true self anymore. We cannot change that which we do not recognize.

We all have had moments when we have reacted to a situation in a certain way, then later silently asked ourselves, "Why did I do that?" or "Why did I say that?" Unfortunately, most of the time we simply shrug it off and console ourselves with, "that was weird". In order to change that response, we need to identify it and bring into question where it comes from. Researchers believe they are able to measure a person's happiness even though it is such a subjective feeling. Their evaluation will be based on the individuals reporting the level of happiness they are feeling at the time. I for one do not think this is scientifically accurate.

It is akin to the chart hospitals use when they ask you the level of pain you are experiencing. You pick a number from 1 to 10 to rate your pain level. This is neither accurate nor reliable since the subjectivity of pain is so individual.

A person with a broken arm that has a low threshold of pain may report it as a 10 and get pain medication based on this response. Meanwhile, a person with the same broken arm and a high threshold of pain may rate it a 6. The reaction to that level is not going to be the same as the 10, so this person experiencing the same pain is less likely to get the same level of pain medication.

Happiness is all in the attitude and approach we take in our daily lives. If we focus on the good in others, and especially in ourselves, then we will have a positive outlook and maintain a positive frame of mind.

When we are confronted with a negative event, we are more apt to rebound from it faster and more positively if we have taught ourselves to refocus on the good in everything about us and our life.

Our happiness starts inside and is maintained by us and only us. We are the masters of our mind, and as such, can choose happiness and joy to guide us though life.

Why Does That Make Me Feel Unhappy?

In 2009, I broke my back in two places when I fell 12 feet off my patio. It was an exceptionally tough time in my life. I spent 6 weeks in the hospital. When I went home, I had to wear a plastic brace that caused my grandson to call me, "My Mutant Ninja Turtle Papa".

There was no position I could get comfortable in, and the possibility for returning to work was just about nil. Altogether, I had 6 surgeries and countless procedures in an effort to return some level of quality to my life.

In 2012, I had a Neuro-Stimulator implanted at the base of my spine to try and alleviate some of the pain. It worked to relieve enough pain that I no longer needed to take the strong pain medications. This was a huge part of the battle to get some quality back in my life.

I was forced into early retirement. I'd had a career in sales for almost thirty years, and my much restricted mobility made it impossible for me to continue in that line of work. But that was all I knew how to do for my livelihood. It was not work to me. I truly loved being in sales.

So now I was forced not only to deal with the loss of my livelihood, but also to endure a much restricted lifestyle that was foreign to me. Just a few years prior, this would have been totally inconceivable. But here I was, in a place I never thought I would be in without the personal resources to help me cope.

Financially I was okay, but my psyche was about as bankrupt as I ever thought possible. Depression had taken over and was digging the hole I was in deeper with each passing day. I justified this self-imposed mental prison by constantly repeating to myself how it was so unfair for this to happen to me. I was trapped in that "Why Me" cycle of self-pity.

I remained in this cycle for almost a year. When I finally started to find my way out, I honestly think it began with a small accident my grandson had. He was nine years old at the time and had hurt his ankle while playing in the yard with his father. He came in crying and sat in the living room with me.

He finally stopped crying and left the room to go outside again, or so I thought. About twenty minutes later, I looked down the hall and saw him sitting quietly in the family room. I asked him what he was doing. He said, "I hurt myself like you, Papa, so I'm sitting here alone like you do." Ah, from the mouths of babes.

This started me thinking about what I was doing. The psychologist said I was depressed, so naturally I focused on being depressed. My grandson said I was unhappy, and yes, it made me think of what I was doing to myself. I was, by clinical definition, depressed, but I realized that all that diagnosis did for me was draw my focus on a condition I had previously thought beyond me.

I acquired an acute sense of tunnel vision and every waking thought was on how bad my condition was; nothing else mattered. Now, a simple statement by a child had penetrated the wall of despair I had erected for myself. Each day I was able to bring myself closer to who I am and away from who I had become. One brick at a time, if you will.

I began to realize that although I was restricted in my life in terms of physical limitations, I had no limitations on my mind and spirit. In those areas, I was still the person I was before the accident.

I realized how much I had allowed my spiritual well-being to be affected by uncontrollable circumstances. My ability to feel and experience happiness was so clouded by all that had happened, that I failed to realize that it was still alive and well inside me. I had lost my true self.

This made me think of all the times in my life when I had allowed my happiness to be affected by circumstances or outside forces. I finally saw that my happiness was all a state of mind. It was the fact that I chose that state of mind, not anyone or anything else. I couldn't do the work I had done my whole life, but I could do the work I dreamed about doing my whole life -writing to help others find a happier life for themselves. We are the masters of our minds. Only we decide what makes us happy or sad. It is our thoughts that determine our state of mind.

All our emotions are guided by the state of mind we are in at any given time. Our state controls all emotions and thoughts, and our thoughts control our state of mind. Therefore, our thoughts are the masters of our life. If we chose to think negative thoughts, we will reap negative results.

A great philosopher, James Allen, once said:

"Of all the beautiful truths pertaining to the soul which have been restored and brought to light in this age, none is more gladdening or fruitful of divine promise and confidence than this - that man is the master of thought, the molder of character, and maker and shaper of condition, environment, and destiny."

These words speak the utmost truth of thought. We must realize that we control our thoughts, and as such control our destiny. If we choose good thoughts of joy and happiness, then we will see more joy and happiness in life all around us.

Have you ever noticed that when you buy a new car, it all of a sudden seems as though there are more of them on the road than you previously saw? Of course, there are no more; the difference is that now your thoughts are on that particular car so you are seeing more. There has not been a change in their numbers, but a change in what you see.

It is the same with happiness. The happier you are, the more people around you seem happier. Your state of joy is opening your eyes to see more joy in others, and showing your happiness is allowing others to see and share in it with you. It is the same as someone smiling at you; you smile back without giving it any thought. The average person smiles about seven times a day, but a happy person smiles about eleven times a day and a grumpy person only once. Which one are you?

What Is Forgiveness?

We go through our lives stuck with the inevitable truth that we must interact with people each and every day. This includes people with a myriad of different religions, cultures, beliefs, and different concepts of respect, friendship, family, and self.

And it would be a perfect world for all to understand and accept all. But, we live in as imperfect a world as can be imagined in terms of differences in beliefs in all aspects of our lives. There are cultures that believe their God is the only acceptable God, people that insist their way is the only way, and as diverse a group of others in between that we can possibly imagine.

We all know we have a spirit of free-will inside of us. No person can make us think or act in a way we choose not to, but is that the way we actually behave? Is it truly a free will, or are we acting the way we have been "taught" to act?

As sure as the sun rises, we will have conflicts, disagreements, and ideals thrust upon us that counter who we are and what we believe. So what do we do in these situations? How do we handle a situation when we are angered or hurt, or when we anger or hurt another?

While growing up, most of us have been taught that we must forgive and forget. We were also taught how to forgive. We learned Mom and Dad's way, how our siblings handled it, and even the many different ways our friends responded to the process.

The word "forgive" means, 'to cease to have feelings of anger or bitterness toward', but it also means, 'to dismiss as of little importance'. So, which do we choose? Do we deal with being angry, or shrug it off as not important? These are the questions I hope to bring some clarity to. And the answers are not as clear cut as you would think.

Forgiveness plays a very big part in feeling happy. Carrying the burden of not forgiving someone, or ourselves, keeps us locked into the past and doesn't allow us to live in the moment. We carry this with us and, whether consciously or not, allow it to affect our level of happiness. The joy of forgiving is an internal happiness that we can truly call our own. In order to better understand forgiving, we must look back to our belief systems and find how we have been taught to forgive and decide if it's the way we want to deal with forgiving as the person we are today.

How Our Beliefs Affect Forgiveness

The best place to begin looking at forgiveness is our beliefs. The key to our understanding why we hold beliefs or values contrary to some of those around us is to understand just what a belief system is. It is the psychological state that holds us to believe a premise to be true without any factual basis for that premise.

We are exposed to so many beliefs as children that it would be impossible to list them all here. Let me list a few of the more simple and common ones so it is a bit clearer:

- Dragonflies sew your lips shut.
- Swallowing a watermelon seed will make it grow in your stomach.
- Thunder is the sound of God bowling.

As simple as these may sound, some believe these to be true into their adulthood, and continue teaching them to their children. As children, we hold strength in the words adults tell us to be true. We rely on their words and teachings to keep us safe. These beliefs have an early beginning in a time in our lives when we are the most susceptible to hold them as true and factual.

This principle has even more power of endurance when the area of superstitions is involved. Think about the superstitions you hold. Here are a few of the more common ones:

- Walking under a ladder is bad luck.
- Breaking a mirror is 7 years of bad luck.
- A black cat crossing your path is bad luck.

Of course there is the flip side to these negative superstitions as well:

- A rabbit's foot brings good luck.
- Finding a 4 leaf clover is good luck.
- Finding a penny heads up is good luck.

I would be remiss if I didn't mention the impact technology and social media has on these superstitions. We are all subjected to the myriad of postings that claim to bring good things, even from God, if you send something to 5 friends in 5 minutes. The truth be told, these are most often started by people or companies that are building lists of names and information for their own marketing or to sell.

They use the power of these superstitions to lure people into doing their bidding. It is a much cheaper proposition for them to fool people into unwittingly collecting the information for them, than it is to pay for the information. And we oblige them to the point that some will even say that if you do not pass it on then you will have some form of bad luck. This is the power we surrender to our belief systems each and every day of our lives.

What can we do to change this scenario? We need to look at our core values, the guiding principles we live by, our fundamental values. What makes us act the way we do in certain situations?

The values we live by all have triggers that automatically bring to the forefront our learned behavior and beliefs in any given situation. An example of a trigger may be a song you heard when you were in a highly emotional state.

Now whenever this song plays you immediately associate that particular emotional happening to that song and you return to that emotional state. This is all done at a subconscious level; the entire process is very autonomic.

If we are to change our "programmed" way of reacting in various situations, then we must first identify what we want to change, as well as identify the trigger or anchor that flips the switch causing us to react as we did. This will be a somewhat easy challenge for some beliefs, and not so much for others.

I want to present you with an example of how embedded a belief can become. When you were an infant growing into a toddler, the bulk of your learning was visual. You learned how certain actions would make you cry or laugh, but you also learned a more complex set of triggers that were based on the interpretation of body language and facial actions.

For example, if you fell and hurt yourself, someone would come running to see that you were okay. What you learned was that how you will be treated when your "rescuer" arrives depends on who comes.

You learn that Mommy means you will be picked up and cuddled, often getting your boo-boo kissed to make it feel better. On the flip side, when Daddy comes, you learn that he will pick you up, look at your boo-boo and tell you that you'll be okay and that it's not that bad. So now you know to go to Mommy for whatever hurts.

Another grand belief we are taught is through our siblings. Your brother and sister are playing out in the yard. You are with Mom at the sandbox watching. Your brother falls and hurts his knee. He has latched onto the Mom thing you learned and comes over crying. Mom takes him in the house and fixes his boo-boo. He is told to stay in for a little so this injury will stop hurting.

Now, your sister falls off her bike. You watch, waiting for her to cry and come to Mom, but she doesn't. She gets up, wipes off her pants, and looks at her knee. "I'm okay," she yells and goes on riding her bike.

You have two anchors before you. Your brother who is sitting in the house not playing, or your sister who is still out having fun. Can you see the power this will have on how you will adapt to the boo-boo's of your life?

Our parents play a major role in our lives when we are young, from two to seven years old in particular. Our personalities are formed based on their teachings. This includes how we react to being hurt both physically and emotionally.

We watch and learn from how they react to our siblings, how they act between each other, and especially how they respond to any form of crisis. Which beliefs we choose to adopt is based on the influence that person has and the number of times we experience a particular action.

I've been giving the simplest examples, but there are many more powerful examples of beliefs that we carry into our adulthood. A more universal belief would be whether or not we believe in God, how we do it, what we need in life to be happy, and even our attitude about money.

If you were to actually sit down and write down the beliefs you have, I think you would be astounded at the number of items you will be putting down on the piece of paper.

Understanding our beliefs is paramount to understanding our behavior in any given situation. As adults, we seldom question our reasons for how we react to various events in our lives.

Our beliefs work quietly in the background. There is no fanfare or desire to question them. You simply react because, "I've always been like this." If we are to analyze them, first we must come to the realization that they exist. Then, we must look at them in depth to try and discover their origins.

Without this vital first step, there is little chance of us recognizing them as a learned behavior and hence, no chance of deriving their origination and changing those we chose to change.

This single step is the single most important move in understanding our personal attitude about forgiving others and our ability to forgive. So stop and take a look at yourself throughout your life. Remembering those times of hurt that stand out from any other:

- That first time you were dumped.
- When you and your best friend had that huge argument.
- When a close family member did something to really hurt you.

Thinking of these moments will open your mind to many other less-significant times when forgiving or being forgiven played a role in your life.

You should begin to see a pattern that probably started as a young child. You will be amazed at how many thoughts you just can't justify.

There is an old adage that says, "Birds of a feather flock together". This is truer than most of us realize. Our thoughts become more like those around us the longer we are around them. We all like to say that we are an individual and can think for ourselves. For the most part, this is true throughout our adult life.

But, as we were growing up we more easily adopted the thoughts of the group we associated with. We are born with the need to belong. One of our biggest challenges as we grow is to *fit in*. I know when each of us looks back to those early teen years and even younger, we remember how critical it was to belong to our chosen circle of friends.

Abraham Maslow's "Hierarchy of Needs", probably the most accepted model of human development in the world of psychology, puts the need to belong in the third level of achievement making it as important to our development as love and family.

I know I can recall times when I was younger that I was rejected by my friends for one reason or another. It was the most depressing, lonely feeling a young person will have in their young life. Although we learn to handle this rejection a bit differently as we develop into teenagers and young adults, it is still a very powerful force to handle, even as an adult.

When we were entering this stage of development, we would find ourselves doing whatever was needed to win the group's approval. It was paramount to our self-esteem to win the recognition of those around us.

Think about some of the things you would do such as wearing certain clothing, talking in group lingo not understood by outsiders, smoking, having a drink, or any number of behaviors membership required.

It's a paradox since there was no thought of yourself as an individual; "group think" dominated your thoughts and actions, yet your self-esteem grew and was reinforced by others. Of course, for some this was a more powerful force than for others, depending on the environment and family influences around us.

This is the primary force that makes belonging to a gang so powerful for some. They are accepted for who they are, and as long as they subscribe to the gang's culture, they readily forfeit their individuality for the security and safety of the gang.

Now you are probably asking yourself, "What does this have to do with forgiveness?" Well, since you asked, I'll tell you. Think back to a time in your early teens when you had a group of people that hung around together all the time, your comfort group if you will. Now, think about having a disagreement within the group and how you responded to it, even if it didn't involve you directly. The chances are strong that the things said and the disagreement itself was cleared up quickly, with little regard as to who was right or wrong.

You knew the rest of the group was watching to see how the two people involved handled the situation and whether you realize it or not, it was most likely resolved by adhering to a set of unspoken guidelines the group had established for resolving in-group problems. And as such, you developed your methods of conflict solving. This is dependent on whose methods left the strongest impression on you; the 'group think' or family.

So you have established your guidelines for forgiveness. There was no thought of who influenced your direction, only that you have your way of handling situations of disagreement or conflict. Most likely it is a combination of different influences in your life adapted for you so as to cause the least amount of conflict within your own mind. But now comes a very important question. Are you handling forgiveness in a way that makes you feel good with yourself? Some of us have grown up in a house of conflict, always yelling at each other or name calling, while others have been taught to walk away and perform the proverbial turn of the other cheek. Each of our environments have their own methodologies for resolving conflict.

Our home, social, and work environments each demand a different and unique set of "rules" that help guide us in this area. When we run into problems in any area, it is usually because we are trying to use our methods for home conflict in our social environment for example. The solution to any random problem will differ according to the people involved, as well as many other factors.

Forgiving Others

It is important to remember that forgiveness is a singular action or process. Whether you are forgiving somebody else's mistake, or your own, it is you and only you that can forgive. The expression that every story has two sides is true.

The most difficult part of that truth is actually understanding the other person's position. We have to release ourselves from the emotional link to the situation if we are to have any hope of understanding another's actions.

We must realize that a person acts on any given situation with the resources they have at their disposal at that given time. What I mean is that if the circumstances dictate an emotional overtaking of a person's mind and behavior at the time of the incident, then the behavior is going to be emotionally based and most likely not contain any elements of logic.

So, when I say "understanding another's actions", I mean the context or environment where the action needing forgiveness happens. Fully understanding why someone said or did something is not as important as understanding the possibilities of what could have influenced them to say or do it. We all have times when the "heat of the moment" controls our actions. We all have experienced the regret of our actions after we said or did what we did.

If you look back at some of these times in your life, you will see that most of these instances are emotion based. Almost all of the emotion based ones involve someone we care about to one degree or another. The logic based happening occur with less frequency.

These are the ones when someone, including yourself, takes a stand on an issue and refuses to see the other side of the issue, meanwhile insisting that their position is the only right way to look at it.

Some of these confrontations will become emotional confrontations, but most will be resolved through the presentation of facts, or the agreement between two people who simply agree to disagree. The forgiveness in these matters is usually easier because the contention here is logic-based, and most likely caused by one of the party being misinformed of the facts. Forgiveness is not a feeling we have, and it is not an emotion we feel. It is a choice we make based mainly on circumstance and intention. You must decide if the person you need to forgive hurt you with intent, or when encompassed with emotion.

We must even give consideration to the possibility that we did something to invoke the response that hurt us. When you look at the act of forgiving someone, it is not always as cut and dry as, "They were drunk and didn't know what they were saying."

And of course our level of commitment to that person weighs heavily in our approach to forgiveness. But, make no mistake that the act of forgiving plays a major and ever present role in our lives. How we approach it within ourselves will be a decisive factor in our continued and long term relationships. I am sure that you have heard people say, or maybe even said yourself, "I can forgive what you did, but I'll never forget." If you look at that statement, what the person is really saying is, "You've hurt me really bad, and I don't want *you* to ever forget it."

It is a means to bring a measure to the level of pain or hurt felt, while still maintaining your ongoing relationship with that person. It is important to keep in mind that the act of forgiving does not come with conditions.

You never want to forgive someone and tell them, "If it ever happens again, we won't be friends anymore", or "I can forgive you under one condition". Again, the depth of your relationship with the person plays a key role in forgiveness, but regardless of that forgiveness is from the heart and soul. Like love, forgiveness must stand by itself with no terms or conditions. When we have something happen between us and another, it is important to not jump into the act of forgiving during the heat of the moment. Doing this can have unrealized consequences later that can leave a person feeling doubtful as to whether or not they are forgiving for the right reason.

It is not a question of whether they should they be forgiven, but more an internal feeling of why you are forgiving. What I mean by this is that you must not forgive just for the sake of ending a bad moment. It can leave you feeling resentful towards that person and leave the problem unresolved within yourself.

You always want to forgive out of caring and love, not as a resolution to conflict. This will leave you feeling good about yourself and the other person, with no residual feelings weighing on your mind. Understanding this need to forgive may help provide us with a better grasp of the act of forgiveness itself. Always keep in mind that forgiving is not an act of weakness. Contrariwise, it is an act of love. It should be unconditional so that all in our life can benefit from it.

Forgiving Ourselves

One of the hardest undertakings we as humans have to do is self-evaluation, whether it be in our efforts to change a characteristic we are unhappy with, or a behavior that disturbs us. Trying to evaluate our own behavior is a delicate process. It requires us to accept the reality that we have something wrong or bothersome within.

To accomplish this subjectively requires us to acknowledge that we are vulnerable and less than perfect. Although some will find it easier than others, we all have to realize that accepting the fault does not mean we are a bad person. It simply means that we are human, and as such, are imperfect beings. If you have doubts about losing your sense of self in this process, it can help if you think of the reason you need to forgive yourself as a behavior done to you from another. Does the behavior, if done to you, leave you feeling angry, hurt, or troubled?

Is it a behavior you would want others to see in you? These questions can cause you to have a feeling of insecurity since we all have a tendency to connect this type of needed change with a flaw in our personality.

It far better for us to experience a moment of insecurity than to live in conflict with ourselves over a behavior we know is not who we really are. To begin, we must make ourselves understand that forgiving is not a negative action. It is wholly a change in the most positive sense. We are replacing a behavior that has often caused us to experience cognitive dissonance, an inner conflict with our actions going against our beliefs, with a positive action that brings us back into alignment with who we are.

The resulting change will be a happy, even joyful and blissfully gratifying feeling that brings us that special innermost happiness of doing something good for those in our life, including ourselves. Being unable to forgive the self denies us the right to let go of the past and live here and now. If you remember earlier, I talked about behaviors and beliefs. Not forgiving within has the same effect as not changing a belief we have found to be lacking any logical base.

If your Dad showed you something and said, "This is how we always do it," and you found a better and easier way to do the same thing, would you continue to do it like Dad showed you? Of course not! So why would you allow something like forgiving to cloud your mind with the past if you know inside that it needs to be dealt with?

Now, it is important to remember that forgiving does not necessarily mean forgetting. If we allow ourselves to forget, then there is a good chance that we have destined ourselves to repeat the same circumstance and have to deal with it again.

Remember the resolution you arrived at, and you will be positioned to avoid it in the future. Remember it in the positive sense of improving yourself, not in the negative sense of making a mistake.

Remember that you are a human being and, as such, are destined to make mistakes, wrong choices, and occasionally bad actions. This is the way of the world at every level of society and culture.

No one is exempt from the flaws of human nature. No, not even you. Although, I must admit that we all like to think the old saying of, "That would never happen to me," or "I'd never act like that or say something like that." Chances are you have already, or you will in the future.

Accept that, identify it when it happens, and resolve it within to grow.

We all have a problem with accepting the negative emotions we encounter throughout our life: anger, envy, and fear to name a few. They are unavoidable, and as much a part of us as the positive emotions of joy, love, and gratitude. Accepting the negative can bring us inner turmoil, because most think of these emotions as weaknesses.

Imagine how hard it is to deal with these if you have a preeminent personality, where everything must be in distinct order and control. This personality can be quite overpowering and prevent someone from actually forgiving themselves. To do so is to admit to being flawed, a polar opposite to the preeminent personality.

Perfection may seem attainable, but it is not. A person seeking perfection will never reach their goal and will always feel the pangs of non-attainment.

The Negative People In Our Life

Unfortunately, we all have negative people in our lives that we just can't avoid. They try to change us to their standards in many different ways. They are close friends, family members, or coworkers that you must interact with each and every day. So, what do you to avoid getting caught up in that negative circle?

First, you must come to the realization that negative attitudes are cancerous and spread to those around the negative person very fast. Whether we consciously realize it or not, they influence our thinking and we may not even realize that it is happening to us.

The more negative your brain ingests, the less room for positive.

The first thing needed is to recognize when the negative talk is taking over the conversation and avoid getting drawn into the attitude. Excuse yourself to do something, or at least try to change the subject to a more positive thought.

Not wanting to be a part of the negative attitude of someone close to you does not mean that you do not like or care for them. It simply means that you do not want to be pulled into the world of the naysayer. There is nothing wrong with this. Because the more negative you are subjected to, the bigger the chances are that it will overtake the forward positive attitude you have for yourself.

People too weak to change their lives always seek to change yours.

Our actions in our lives will always introduce us to people that are too weak to change their own lives. They may be people close to us that we care about, but make no mistake, some of these people will try to change your life by discounting your position in life and bringing you down to theirs.

Do not hate them for this, or they have succeeded. How many times have you heard such a person say, "She was always lucky," or, "He had everything handed to him."? This is because they must discount any possibility that the person is what they are because of a personal effort to live a happy and positive life.

It is because your positive life reflects poorly on their own. To accept that you yourself are solely responsible for your happiness is to admit that they are solely responsible for the discord of theirs.

"Forgiveness might make us look weak, but the weakest person is the one who holds anger, hatred, and revenge." -- Unknown

Holding On To The Negative

Isn't it amazing how some people will not let go of past mistakes no matter what? Something you said in the heat of an argument two years ago is still held over your head every time you disagree with that person. "Oh, here we go again."

Are you going to insult me again like you did before?" "Don't argue with Jim. He'll just get upset and start calling you names." Every person on earth has made mistakes. Every person on earth knows somebody that will not let them get past those mistakes.

Your natural growth and learning process dictates that you are going to make mistakes along the way. Not *some* of us will and *some* won't; <u>everyone,</u> without exception, has to make mistakes to grow.

It is not the mistakes that matter as much as how you learn and adapt from your mistakes. If we choose to have mistakes attached to us like a ball and chain, then you can be assured that they will drag us down.

It is not up to anyone else to decide when you should be released of the burden of accountability for a mistake; it is up to you.

Daring to venture out is accepting mistakes as part of the growth process.

If anyone denies you support as you grow beyond your mistakes of the past, it becomes their burden to carry, not yours. As cliché as it sounds, the old adage of, 'We must learn from our mistakes.' is the truth to its core.

You must look at the obstacle the mistake has caused you, and remove it so you can continue on the path of growth you have mapped out for yourself. This may sound cold, but if anyone in your life keeps drumming up your past mistakes in an effort to hold you back, it might be time to say goodbye to that person. For those that care and encourage you, your past is gone and they help to shine their light of support on your future.

Another aspect of not living in the shadow of our past mistakes is your own handling of the influence you allow them to have on you. If you have made the mistake of hurting someone close to you, it is imperative that you do not depend on their forgiveness to remedy the wrong.

If you have said you are sorry and that is not enough to appease them then there is nothing more you can do. The next crucial step is to forgive yourself and move on. This is surprisingly easily done by acknowledging the mistake, understanding how it can be avoided in the future, and putting it behind you so it no longer remains an obstacle before you.

Most family and friends will accept your apology and maintain the healthy relationship you have always had with them. To those that won't, they are the ones making the mistake now.

If You Aren't Making Mistakes, You Aren't Growing

If I chose to list the mistakes I've made in my life, this article would become a book. However, I also know that those mistakes have made me who I am today.

Each one has caused a small change in the strategy I had planned for myself. So make your mistakes. Do not deny them; use them to get a better understanding of who you are and who you want to be tomorrow.

Remember those who consistently point out your mistakes are the ones so desperately seeking to raise themselves above those around them. Since they cannot do it through their own merits, they must seek to lower others for the appearance of themselves being better. You will know your friends as the ones that point out a mistake, but also enjoy the good in your successes.

Being Your Own Worst Enemy

Sometimes it is not the people around you that you need to worry about. We all have our own personal demon that will feed us criticism just as readily as anybody out there. There is one big difference in how you must deal with it when it is internal.

Since you cannot simply leave the room to get away, you have to meet this fiend head on – no pun intended– and decide how to eliminate it. Of course, I am referring to our penchant for criticizing our self At times, this critique is much stronger and more relentless than any another person could give.

Self-criticism can present a serious challenge to your personal development. What can make it even worse than another criticizing us is that you may not even realize that you are being your own worst enemy.

You may tell yourself that you are being hard on yourself because you want more out of life; you want to grow and succeed. Wanting more from life is fine. It is the force that drives you to try different things and to make yourself better than you are at any given moment.

Questioning one's self is the death blow to certainty.

However, it can also be what is holding you back, or at the least making the journey slower and harder than it has to be. The effect of persistent self-criticism is not as simple as "being hard on yourself." It is silently and, in most cases, not noticeably causing self-doubt to rear its ugly head.

Self-doubt is the enemy of growth. It causes uncertainty in your decision making and makes taking that next step forward a lot tougher. Certainty is what allows you to take that next step without hesitation or worry.

Self-doubt erodes your level of certainty. It gives you pause as to whether or not you should even take that step. I am not talking about being certain about the results of your next move, but rather being certain about the need to make the move to advance yourself one step closer to your goal. The certainty comes in knowing you will handle the results whatever they may be.

Abraham Maslow was an American psychologist. He was best known for creating Maslow's Hierarchy of Needs, a theory of psychological health based on fulfilling innate human needs in priority, culminating in self-actualization.

His first level is the basics we need of physical survival: food, water, and air. The next level is called Safety and includes our need for security, limits, and order. This is the level that can bring the strongest challenge to your psyche. Embracing the three needs I mentioned too firmly can hold you back from taking chances and *going for it*. There are only two choices here:

You can remain in the safety of your current position and accept your current limits as the direction of your life. Or, you can look ahead and step into the unknown, knowing that you have yet to see the limits of your growth, and move yourself forward. Remember one of the primary definitions of challenge is to demand as due or deserved.

At any given moment in life, you are the culmination of your thoughts. A great philosopher, James Allen, once wrote, "As he thinks, so he is; as he continues to think, so he remains."

His book, *As a Man Thinketh*, is very deep at times. As you read it you will find many of his thoughts to be true. If you want to download a free PDF the link is here.

Oh! The Drama

Oh the drama of it all! We all know people and have friends that live in the soap opera world of drama and chaos, where the culmination of one bizarre event simply opens the door to another. It is a never ending cycle, and the life blood to the TV soap.

However, we also have drama queens and kings in our personal lives as well. Whether they are family, friends, or co-workers, they feed on drama to the point where they strive to produce it from events that would otherwise be mundane and uneventful.

If you approach that person and say, "Did you hear about Susan and Bob?" even though they started the drama scene, they will most often reply, "I know, I heard it from a few people so it must be true."

"Basically, if you're tired of the drama in your life, you need to stop being the actor."

If you know someone like this what do you think of them? Do you admire the drama they produce? Do you help them in their quest to keep the drama alive?

If you can see yourself as this person, you need to make a quick and decisive change in your thought process, regardless of whether you are the drama producer or an agent for the drama producer. It is easy to identify either role within yourself if you pause and look at situations where you have participated. However, identifying this problem is much easier than solving it.

It requires you take an honest and open look at your role in the drama. You must see how you contribute, and then find the next step to change that.

There are two ways to go about the necessary change. One is if you sit at the table and have a drama person eating with you, let them eat alone. If a person approaches you and you immediately know it is time for your drama lesson from them, make excuses that you do not have time to hear their story.

Or, you can come right out and be honest. In a friendly way, tell them that you are not interested. This way is blunt, but it almost guarantees that you will not hear any more stories.

The second way, and least likely way to offend anyone, is also the simplest; be patient, hear their story, and keep your mouth shut. Once they have told their tale, do not waste any of your precious thought processes on it and forget you ever heard it.

The only people that like drama in their lives, usually at other's expenses, are those with mundane and uneventful lives of their own. These are people that get much needed attention at the cost of their own character.

Do not be dramatic. Do not listen to drama. And above all, do not become the actor in other's soap operas.

"The number of times you say you hate drama is directly proportional to the number of times you start it."

Self-Esteem

Self-esteem is probably the most difficult disposition a person will have to deal with in their pursuit of a happier and more fulfilling life. Many use the term self-esteem and self-consciousness as interchangeable. Although they are closely associated, there is a difference.

Self-consciousness is generally used in terms of a physical disparity one feels about their body or appearance. Self-esteem is generally used to reference one's emotional evaluation of their self-worth. It is a judgment of a person's own worthiness placed on his or her self.

Nathaniel Branden, a psychotherapist who's work focused on self-esteem, best describes it as, "The sum of self-confidence (our feelings of personal ability) and self-respect (our feelings of personal integrity)."

It exists on the premise that all humans have the ability to understand and solve their daily problems, and the right to achieve happiness. So in simplistic terms, self-esteem means, "How do I feel about myself today?"

Low self-esteem can be a serious issue for some. We all have moments when our self-esteem can be low on a short term basis (i.e. when you have done something that hurts someone close to you). As a long term condition, it can lead to depression, affect our social interactions, and hinder our ability to feel compassion.

Constant episodes of low self-esteem will manifest to low self-worth. (I'll discuss this further down.) This can cause you to get entangled mentally in two cognitive conditions: perfectionism and self-degradation.

Perfectionism causes you to keep yourself to a higher standard that is impossible to maintain since perfection simply does not exist. It is not possible to reach a level of satisfaction with "being perfect" because you are always striving to be a bit better than a moment ago. This makes it an impossible goal to reach. Self-degradation, or putting yourself down, can be part of perfectionism.

Instead of accepting the unattainability of perfectionism, you blame yourself for not reaching it. You set an impossible goal and feel weak and unworthy when you cannot reach it.

So what is the solution? To start, you have to accept the fact that you are human. As such, you fall and stumble, and you rise and soar. This is life. Everybody experiences these ups and downs. It is what you do with these on a personal level that determines their effect on you.

If you are struggling with a problem at work for instance, do not let it become a personal issue. It may be that you do not have the proper resources provided to you, or it may be that you do not yet have the adequate training to be able to deal appropriately with the situation.

You are not having these issues because you are not a good enough person or because you have a character flaw. It is not about you as a person. It is important to remember that the hurdles we face, and we all face them, are the process of growing and not a test of who we are as a person on an emotional level.

In order to discover and deal with the issue of low-esteem, it is important for you to reach inside yourself and discover what parts you are unhappy with. It may be something that developed as a child. The way our parents accepted us when we were small has a great influence on how we accept ourselves now as adults.

Remember, as a child you were much more susceptible to feeling low-esteem because you were so dependent on your parents approval to feel good about yourself. The praise you received from your parents was totally dependent on the way you acted. From that you *learned* what behaviors are okay and which are not. When we identified ourselves with the not okay behaviors, we would begin to feel unsatisfactory about ourselves.

For some of us this feeling of being unsatisfactory stayed with us into adulthood. Your childhood experiences guide you in one way or another to this day. Identify the ones that are holding you back and change them to fit the person you are now. Know that, as an adult, you require only self-approval to feel happy about anything. Identifying them is as easy as saying to yourself, "Why do I feel bad when I do ___?".

Our self-esteem is directly related to our happiness. I am talking about the natural happiness we feel inside about our self, our life, our family, and our friends, not the temporary happiness we feel when we get a raise, or win money. Those are good feelings but because they are brought on by external factors, they are temporary.

True happiness comes from within. It is from seeing the good in our self and our life. It is the feeling we get when we help another and bring them a smile. It is that special feeling of love and warmth we have when we are surrounded by family and friends.

Self-worth and self-esteem, although closely related, are very different in one very important aspect. Self-esteem is based on single events in your life while self-worth is based on your love and understanding of self.

For instance, if you are having a hard time at work or in a relationship, this can affect your self-esteem. But, if you continue to have these instances affecting your self-esteem, they will begin to affect your self-worth. You will begin to doubt your worthiness as a person and your personal value of yourself.

This is why it is so very important to get an understanding with yourself that the mistakes, poor choices, or failures you experience are all singular events. They are not the sum of who you are.

We all experience these throughout our lives and as cliché as it may sound, they are the foundation of our triumphs and successes in life. We will occasionally get lucky and find out what is right the first time around, but more often than not, we will find what is right by experiencing and eliminating what is wrong first.

Accept that you, like every other human being, are imperfect. Accept that, just as when you were a young child, you will fall many times before you walk successfully. Know that your stumbles in life are lessons on what not to do and nothing more.

You have within you the love, compassion, and spirit we are all born with. Cultivate that and you will always know the joy of living and the value you have to everything and everyone around you, including yourself.

Does Self-Esteem Really Exist?

I see self-esteem not as a single condition of one's mind, but more the catch-all phrase for many conditions of the mind including: self-worth, self-respect, confidence, and integrity. To me, low self-esteem is the result of one or more of these conditions being absent or in low regard.

Operating on this premise, it can be easy to see just how complicated the personal evaluation of one's self could be when using self-esteem as the challenge. A person may well have a high level of confidence without placing much self-worth on themselves. What I mean is that a person could well have the confidence to accomplish a given task, but even upon completion they still feel a low level of self-worth.

People suffering from low self-esteem have a tendency to live in the moment. Everything they do now, in the present, will have an impact on them. And, even if it is something positive, they lack the ability to carry the positive experience into the future with them. They will look at the experience and say something like, "Big deal! I got one thing right all day."

I think if we break down the different aspects of self-esteem, it will become a much less daunting task to get our self-pointed in the right direction. It is the same way you would approach a large math problem. There is a set of rules for the order of operations needed to be done in order to reach the right answer. Try to do the problem without breaking it down, and unless you are very lucky, you will not have the right answer in the end.

Take the challenge of self-esteem with the same mindset. Break it down into its parts and focus on a single aspect until you feel comfortable that you are on your way to changing for the happier.

By facing the challenge one step at a time, you are setting smaller goals to reach. As you reach each goal, you will find the next to be easier. Reaching small goals will build your mind up to a positive viewpoint. Before you know it, you will have changed your way of thinking about things to a more compassionate fulfilling point of view.

Remember as a child how frustrating and difficult it was to try and build something with your blocks or log set? Do you also remember how it became like a second nature for you once you did it a few times?

It is the same with our mind now. If you do the little things over and over, they become a natural process of thought and no longer require you to think about them; they become natural. Good thoughts just happen.

When Does Self-Esteem Begin?

Just as our belief systems start their development in our early years, the foundation for how we perceive ourselves in our mind's eye, as well as how we think others view us, develops in our childhood days. The influences of those around us, our parents and playmates more than anyone else, plays a huge role in how we feel about our self.

Our childhood experiences have the strongest input into whether our self-esteem will be positive or negative. The image we develop is based on our interactions with many different people and events in our early life. How we interact during the play times of our childhood are probably the strongest influence on our self-esteem with our parents being a very close second.

If we receive praise when it is due, get the attention we need, are shown love and affection, and are accepted when we make mistakes, then we will have a strong foundation for a positive self-esteem. On the other hand, if we are ridiculed, unduly criticized, are abused in any number of ways, or expectations placed on us by others are too high, then we will look badly upon our self and suffer with low self-esteem. We will feel like a failure, unable to bring happiness to others, and unhappy with ourselves.

These past experiences, whether positive or negative, become instilled inside our minds. They become a subconscious force in our lives as we grow older. We sometimes never understand why we feel the way we do. We may never realize that it is from our childhood. Therefore, we carry on with our life accepting that we are flawed and feeling as though "this is the hand God dealt me."

If you drive to work the same route every day, it becomes burned into your brain. You begin to make the drive without any thought about the direction you are going. The same happens when you are a child. If you are yelled at or punished every time you do something wrong, then you start to believe that this is the way it is in life so you'd better not make any mistakes.

Making a mistake becomes a powerful negative in your mind. When you do something wrong you may deny it to avoid the punishment or ridicule that goes along with it. You lose any sense of responsibility for your mistakes and try to pass the blame to someone else.

As you get older, this translates into an irresponsible person whom others do not trust. Both of these conditions manifest in your self-esteem, and as a result, you in return do not trust others and think others to be the irresponsible ones.

Many of us never realize we are feeling this way. The conditions for it are our subconscious efforts that we were taught as a child. We can go through life thinking this is just how it is, and there is nothing to be done about it.

Self-Worth

Many use the terms self-worth and self-esteem interchangeably. I look at self-worth as being a part of the whole. It groups along with self-respect and self-confidence. Self-worth is something we are all born with an abundance of.

As life progresses, there are many factors that direct us to higher or lower levels. People's attitudes toward us, what they expect from us, and how they talk to us all effect our self-worth in one direction or the other.

Self-worth is how we look at ourselves in terms of other people's values placed on us. As we are growing, we rely heavily on outside opinions, criticisms, and evaluations to form our own views on self-worth. These become the base or foundation of our personal level of self-worth.

> "Sometimes the hardest part of the journey is believing you're worthy of the trip." -Glenn Beck

There are many ways for an individual to build their self-worth. I am going to touch on a few I think are vital to changing the way we look at ourselves.

Since self-worth is the value we see in ourselves, we must first discover exactly how we feel about ourselves. Get alone in a room with a mirror. I suggest using a recorder (most phones can record) rather than writing because writing requires more thought than speaking. In this exercise you must be thinking only of yourself.

First, I want you to look in the mirror and think of the good things you know about yourself. These are the qualities others have said they see in you. Speak them, do not just think them. Talk in the first person, "I am, I have," etc. Let this come out in a natural flow. Do not give it a lot of thought.

Second, speak of the qualities you see in yourself. Whatever it is, say it. These are your own opinions of you. Now you have a sampling of your good traits from the point of view of yourself and others.

> "The mind is everything. What you think you become." - Buddha

Third, think of the things others have said to you that annoy them. The reason for this is to show both sides of the coin. Also, speak of the items you feel inside that you would like to change.

You now have a quick list of self-worth items. Sit down and write out your list so it is available to you at all times. It is very important to remember that the items on the somewhat negative side do not determine your self-worth by themselves.

We all have things about us that can be annoying to others or even to ourselves. I want you to focus on the positive qualities which outnumber the others. I say to focus on them because as you look at your list, you will find the annoying side is made up of characteristics that generally expose themselves during times of stress or anger.

Before worrying about them, it is imperative to focus on the foundation of your self-worth, the value you have as a human being. I know when I made my list I was surprised at the good things I found out about myself. I also found myself saying, "You know, you can be a pain in the ass when it comes to ___."

The good traits made me feel very gratified inside. I learned that I was a much nicer and positive person with myself than I ever realized.. These positives are what attract people to you. You owe it to others, and yourself to build on them.

Positive Thinking?

Positive thinking is one of the most misunderstood concepts of improving one's life. At face value, people look at it as simply thinking of the good things you want and those things coming to you.

If you focus all your energy on a desired outcome, it will manifest itself in your life. The truth is positive thinking is of no use to anyone unless it is accompanied by positive action.

You can look at your garden and keep saying, "No weeds. No weeds." But, unless you do something to prevent weeds, your garden will be overtaken by them. Action is the key to successful positive thinking.

> "Why should we worry about what others think of us, do we have more confidence in their opinions than we do our own?" -Brigham Young

To generate the positive results you want, you must put emotion into the equation. Emotion is the catalyst for any action we take in our life. Everything we decide we are going to do in our life is the result of an emotion attached to the action.

Going out to dinner, to a movie, or to a party all must have positive emotions attached to them if we are to have fun and want to do it. If you do not like going to the movies, then your emotional response will not be happy or enthusiastic. If no positive emotion is assigned, then no positive reaction results.

There has been a lot of writing on, "The Power of Positive Thinking", some of which has taken it to the extreme. It is not some mystical concept or some magical extraction from the universe.

The pop-psychology books that this "power of positive thinking" surge has created has caused us to look at positive thinking as a sort of magical elixir that will cure all our problems. It is powerful enough to change our lives, but it is not magical in the same sense as pixie dust or potions.

"You're always with yourself, so you might as well enjoy the company."
-Diane Von Furstenberg

The magical part is the result that is attainable for anyone choosing to use positive thinking as a tool to a happier life. It is within each of us to change whatever we have the passion to change. We are all born with happiness instilled. Some of us have lost that natural level of happiness and are seeking to find it again. Some of us are confused as to exactly what will bring us the happiness we desire, and some of us have become too dependent on outside circumstance to provide us with happiness.

So how do we get ourselves in the mindset of using positive thinking to help us to a better happier life? Let's look at that now.

How Does It Affect Me?

For the most part, psychology has always dealt with the problems an individual is facing and looked at the cause for those problems. In 1996, Dr. Martin Seligman began a new era in the approach of psychology with positive psychology.

He was elected as the president of the American Psychological Association and chose positive psychology as his theme while in office. This opened a new branch of psychology where the focus was not on the problem, but on how to be happy and more positive about your life.

His focus on what made people feel happy and fulfilled in their life was the start of what is now the positive thinking movement. Instead of looking at what is wrong and how to fix it, positive psychology looks at what is right and how we can enhance it.

Studying happy people and understanding the why's and how's of their happiness has allowed us to get a clearer picture of ourselves and what we need to do to be fulfilled in our lives.

"When you're different, sometimes you don't see the millions of people who accept you for what you are. All you notice is the person who doesn't."
-Jodi Picoult

It is everyone's goal to be as happy and fulfilled as they can be, and it is within the grasp of all of us to find our path to happiness. All it involves is refocusing and taking control of our state of mind at any given time. It is making happiness and joy the journey, not the goal.

Controlling our state of mind is much easier than most people realize. Have you ever had a terrible headache, one that takes you completely out of the game? Most of us have at one time or another.

The headache is so bad that it is all you can focus on. Everything else at that moment is secondary. You are in the zone of this all-encompassing pain. Now one of the children runs into the house crying hysterically, with blood coming from a wound they just got outside, perhaps a knee cut or a fat lip. You jump up to help them and evaluate the extent of the damage. Now your focus is completely on the wounded child. All of a sudden, without you even thinking about it, your headache is not there while you are tending to the child.

> "It's not what you say out of your mouth that determines your life, it's what you whisper to yourself that has the most power!" -Robert T. Kiosaki

The human brain, with all its power, can only focus on one cognitive thought at a time. Any activity that requires your brain to think of the actions you are taking requires all the focus on that activity, hence as in the previous example you are now refocused on your child's situation. Psychology uses this state to help children with pain issues or chronically ill children. It is called distraction therapy. They use toys and games to get the child refocused on the fun activity and not thinking about the pain. The pain is still there, but the brain cannot see it because it is busy on something else.

We can use this same strategy to help us make changes in our thinking. If we make a commitment to change our state of mind to a more positive one, we can then, through constant effort, change our way of thinking. I am not sure who said this, but it is a truth we need to follow:

"Watch your thoughts; they become words.

Watch your words; they become actions.

Watch your actions; they become habits.

Watch your habits; they become character.

Watch your character; it becomes your destiny."

What Can I Do About It?

If we are to bring change into our lives, it is imperative that we first identify that which we want to change. I have found that the best way to identify the changes we want to make is by writing them down. Write the changes on the left side of the paper. On the right side, write the things you are happy with in your life.

Take some time to do this in a quiet and uninterrupted space. This is not a onetime exercise. Anytime during the day you think of something, make a note so you can add it to your self-evaluation list.

> **"Those who cannot change their minds cannot change anything - George Bernard Shaw**

Please do this exercise. If you are serious in your quest for a happier life, then you must make a full commitment. Put yourself into a state of mind that will make the changes you desire easier to implement. If you identify, you can change.

One of the most important first steps you can take is to get a good night's sleep. This means no radio, television, or light. When you have the television on while in bed it is a constant source of attention for your brain.

Each time the screen changes from dark to light, or the voices change volume, your brain, by natural selection, alerts itself to those changes. This keeps you brain from relaxing and allowing itself to slip off into a sleep state. This hinders REM sleep, which is essential for rest of the mind and body.

Now, I know the first thing you are going to say, "I can't sleep unless the television is on." That is just not true. What makes it true for you is that you have assigned it as a belief and now you are convinced that it is necessary to your sleep.

Well, it is not. It is what we talked about earlier, our belief system. At one time in your life, you slept without the TV. But, you have been watching TV in bed for so long now that you think it is needed to get to sleep.

"Once you accept your limits, you'll know how to go beyond them."-James Monty

All that is needed to go to sleep is a quiet area and darkness. These are the natural conditions to getting to sleep and getting the most of a restful night's sleep. This will be one of the easiest things for you to change because it will only require two or three nights without the TV to show that it is better without it.

The trick is to lay down and think about what a great day tomorrow is going to be. After all, it is the first day of the rest of your life. Another trick to use, if your mind wanders to all different thoughts, is to think about your breathing.

Count your breaths. Work on slowing them down. Put all of your focus on this, and you will see how fast you fall to sleep. I actually listen to a rain CD every night, and I fall asleep very quickly. There are no thoughts or concerns of the day, just focused breathing and hearing the rain.

If you have thoughts coming in, refocus them on the strides you have made towards being a happier person. Everything, no matter how small, that you do toward your goal of improvement is a step in the right direction.

Our Right To Be Happy

An 'Inborn Right to Happiness' exists in all of us. Some have lost their way through circumstances and events in their lives that has put their essential right of happiness in the back of their minds.

We need to clean out the clutter that keeps us from finding who we really are and from discovering the true nature of ourselves. You are a happy and joyous person that lives each day for its greatest potential to make others and ourselves better people.

"There is only one cause of unhappiness: the false beliefs you have in your head, beliefs so widespread, so commonly held, that it never occurs to you to question them." - Anthony de Mello

Remember back when you were a child and how easy it was to bring happiness to your life. A new toy, a lollipop or ice cream was all it took to bring a smile into your life. As we grow, life gets a bit more complicated and we forget the simple things.

Bring the simple things back into your life. Rejoice in the feeling of a laugh with a friend, the first lick of your favorite ice cream cone, or the laugh you share with others over some silly little thing. You will make a better world for yourself and anyone that chooses to join you in it.

Is Change Really That Easy?

"It's never too late to be who you might have been." - George Eliot

Sometimes in our lives we come across things that seem to be too good to be true, or just so easy that we have a tendency to pass them by. We have all been taught that if it seems too good to be true, then it most likely is and you should back away. However, too good to be true and just too easy are closely tied together in our minds. Too good to be true generally means the simplicity is out of line with the anticipated results. This link between the two will often cause our brains to apply the "too good to be true" rule when whatever it is we want to do that appears to be just too easy. Hence, we find ourselves discarding some things without giving them a closer look.

I believe there are three reasons people have a challenge with affirmations. One is the aforementioned *too easy* concept. Another is that we have heard the term 'positive affirmations', so often that we have assigned them a label that dispels them as some hocus pocus mumbo jumbo type of supposition. We end up finding ourselves approaching positive affirmations with a negative forethought; this is why we need them in the first place. So we have defeated any possible good that can come from them before we have even started.

> "A year from now you will wish you had started today." - Karen Lamb

The third and probably the most prevalent challenge has to be the lack of action that needs to be associated with the positive change. Many articles I have read on positive affirmations fail to emphasize the most important and necessary aspect of the affirmation: **action.** We can sit and repeat an affirmation until we are blue in the face and nothing is going to happen until we put it into action. I look out at my lawn and keep saying, "There are no weeds. There are no weeds". Guess what? I have weeds and will until I do something to prevent them.

Try to think of change you want in your life as avouchment; declare it to be a matter of fact. There is no 'I might' or 'maybe just maybe'. There is only the change you want and the actions to get you there. Your mind is your house; if you do nothing to clean or maintain it, soon it becomes a broken down structure with no semblance of order. So let's start to do some renovations, one simple step at a time.

> "Most folks are about as happy as they make up their minds to be."-Abraham Lincoln

I am going to pick one of the more common changes people want. In my experiences, this is happiness. Now, I know what you are saying, happiness is not a simple task right? But, I want to tell you that it is if taken one step at a time. The great thing about happiness is that it is not a goal. You see and feel results along the way. It is one aspect of our lives that we will always want to have more of and to share more of. So, let's begin with the first step. I think we will start with smiling more. Of course you can chose anything you desire to begin with.

Now smiling is probably one of the most contagious expressions we can show on our face, second only to yawning which I will never understand. Before you go to bed tonight, make a note about smiling where you are absolutely sure you will see it in the morning. When you go to bed I want you to do two things. Sorry to tell some of you, but both are best done in a dark and quiet room. Remember you want to improve so you have to take action. If that means no television at bedtime, make it happen, you deserve it.

First, we are going to do a light meditation. No experience is required. I want you to think about your breathing. You are going to slow it down simply by thinking of it slowing down. Trust me, it works if you honestly do it. You will feel your heart rate slow as well. Now, do not fall asleep yet.

Next, bring to the front of your thoughts how you feel when you are happy and smiling. Think of a time when a natural event in your life just made you smile right to your bones. The first time the baby walked; when you found out that a girl likes you too; or how about the time your boss thanked you for a job well done. Choose a moment that has stayed with you because it felt so good. Now go to sleep. Get a good night's rest and smile the night away. This is the only step you will take to change until you feel it is getting more natural and not requiring thought.

Each day write on a slip of paper how many times you smiled and how many times you made another smile.

Does this sound silly? Maybe, but each day, if you are following through, you will see that number go up. If you are serious about being happier, then you will do it. You will amaze yourself with the power you have over other people's smiles.

> "Sometimes your joy is the source of your smile, but sometimes your smile can be the source of your joy." - Thich Nhat Hanh

Identifying Change Needed

A huge and essential step in identifying the changes we may want or need to make takes us back to our belief system. Many times there is a behavior change you desire that has its roots in your belief system. Let's say you have a habit of talking loudly to speak over someone else talking. This can be irritating to those around you and probably gets you upset when you do it. However it may not be as simple as you being rude, or too anxious to speak that you cannot wait.

I have seen this behavior in many people in my life and have found that it is instilled in them when they were children. You see, they grew up in large families of four or more children close in age. In order for their voice to be heard, they had to speak loudly and most often cut off a sibling's conversation to ensure they were heard

> "Everyone thinks of changing the world, but no one thinks of changing himself." -Leo Tolstoy

As they grow up this becomes part of their belief system, "If you want to be heard you have to say it loud and as soon as you can." Therein lies the problem. They continue to behave this way even though their life's circumstances no longer warrant its necessity. It is the belief system in action. It has become an anchor in their mind and is now an instinctual response rather than a thought out response.

Identifying the changes we want to make requires us to take our search beyond the simple behavior itself and dig for the underlying belief or anchor that triggers that particular behavior. Finding out the root cause is an essential step in our quest to change the things we desire to change. You will be quite amazed at how much easier it is when you have the knowledge of its cause to guide you through the change.

One way to quickly identify if a certain behavior is triggered from your belief system is to think about the times you have heard yourself say, "I've always been like this, I can't change now." If you can link that comment with anything you have done or said, then I can almost guarantee that it is a belief from your childhood you have carried into your adult life, through no fault of your own.

"If you really want to do something, you'll find a way. If you don't, you'll find an excuse." -Unknown

Once you see this you will be delighted at how much easier it is to control that particular behavior, as well as make the necessary changes to eliminate it from your life. When you see someone else displaying the behavior you have just fixed you will find yourself saying, "I used to do that, isn't it annoying?"

When you hear a person who has done some terrible thing say, "It's my parents fault. That's how they brought me up." there is a hint of truth in that. Of course, to blame any other person for your own mistakes is a way for you to cope with the wrong done without looking at yourself as the cause. It is an escape for you to justify what you know inside was your own choice.

Still, our parents and siblings are responsible for most of the beliefs we carry into our adult life. Most of the fears we develop as a child are directly related to our parents' fears. Our attitude for dealing with mistakes has been taught by our parents. There are so many aspects of our behavior linked to the times of our childhood that it would be futile to try to mention them all.

The most important thing to remember here is that no matter what we have as beliefs in our adult life, we are in total control of them. We are the masters of our attitude and behavior regardless of previous teachings. Taking the time to identify and change that which we want changed is a simple matter, although in some instances the change itself is not as easy.

"When you're up, your friends know who you are. When you're down, you know who your friends are."

One final thought on identifying change is that all levels of doubt and uncertainty must be removed before attempting change. It is not an area of your life where you can use terms like, 'I'll try', 'I should be able to', 'maybe I can' or, 'who knows, it might happen'. It is a time when avouchment must rule. This means that you must declare the change to be a matter of fact and not a possibility. Certainty is the force that will bring the change into reality.

Bringing About Change

Now let's tackle actually bringing about the change you want. As mentioned earlier, the first step is identifying the change we want to make. I suggest starting out with something that will be easy for you to implement. The reason is for you to build a solid foundation that you can use for any future changes you engage in.

I am going to use a real life example of this with a change I made in myself some thirty-odd years ago. I grew up as the kid you see sitting on the beach and getting sand kicked in my face. Although in my teen years I weighed in at about 130 lbs. As ridiculous as this sounds, I compensated for that by developing a keen sense of being very quick with the comebacks of the jokes and ridicule I was subjected to.

In other words, I was a smart ass. Sometimes this would get the other person laughing so I did not get my butt kicked. Sometimes it worked the opposite, so I was forced to use my second acquired skill -speedy legs. My mantra in those years was to be sure that no matter who I fought, I always had to inflict some damage that they would remember as they walked away from me lying on the ground in defeat. I was a scrappy sort with a very high tolerance for pain. It must have been somewhat effective since I rarely, if ever, fought the same person more than once.

> "For every minute you are angry you lose sixty seconds of happiness."-Ralph Waldo Emerson

Well, as you can imagine this rather frightening flaw in my character as a teenager did not exactly translate to a positive trait in my young adulthood. For the most part I was accepted as a very funny character. Other times I was projected to be a cruel person, using humor to demean another person.

I can remember exactly the incident that brought this now curse in my character to the forefront of my life. I was 28 years old and I was attending a summer outing for my work. There was this one woman who worked for me in customer service that was rather large and overweight. She was the best customer service representative I had on my team. She always helped others to be better at their jobs.

I was sitting at a picnic table with a few other guys with no females present. We were talking about the different woman in the company, the way 20-something guys would talk. Well, one of my friends said, "You're the lucky one", referring to me, "to have 6 woman working for you. Well, actually 7 if you count Donna as 2 people."

I replied, "It's a good thing her personality is almost as big as her ass. Makes for a great rep, but I can't imagine anything else she'd be great at, if you know what I mean."

"Those who are not looking for happiness are the most likely to find it, because those who are searching forget that the surest way to be happy is to seek happiness for others." -Martin Luther King Jr.

I know I was a cruel ass at the time. I have changed, I promise. As luck would have it, Donna was standing right behind me and heard every word said. I never caught the facial expression of one of the guys. I just blurted out the words. I turned and Donna just gave me a look like it was the end of the world and started crying as she turned to walk away. I was in such shock that I went and added to my ignorance by saying, "She'll get over it. She's a big girl, pun intended."

As I sat there, the level of ignorance I had just exhibited began to overwhelm me. I left the outing shortly after that and went home to consider the consequences of what I had done. I could not figure out why I would have said such a thing. I knew I was not a mean person, although I would tell the occasional joke about someone. I never thought I could be so hurtful.

After sitting at home for a while, it started to dawn on me that I had exhibited the same thoughtless behavior as a teen. Then, it all began to come together. It was a belief system I developed as a defense mechanism and I carried it into my adulthood. How could anyone be so stupid to not recognize this?

> "Children are happy because they don't have a file in their minds called "All the Things That Could Go Wrong." - Marianne Williamson

I was determined to change and stop being inconsiderate and cruel. I would control the words coming out of my mouth. It was not easy to change something as anchored in my mind as this was, but I started my quest to change it with one simple step; I developed a mantra, a word or phrase that is repeated often or that expresses someone's basic beliefs. My mantra was, "If you have nothing good to say about someone, say nothing."

I would repeat this in my head throughout the days to come. Before I knew it, it became my new belief. I do not know exactly how long it took, but I do know that I have succeeded in removing this unwanted behavior from my life.

As far as Donna was concerned, we had lunch together that Monday. I tried to explain myself to her and apologize. Before I could even speak a word she said to me, "That was an ugly side of you I never thought I'd see. I hope you can see just how ugly it is." Indeed I did see; I was fortunate to mend that wrong and we resumed our work relationship as it was before.

Lasting Change

If change is to become a permanent part of your life, it must involve bringing your standards to a higher level. If you remember earlier I wrote:

"Watch your thoughts; they become words.

Watch your words; they become actions.

Watch your actions; they become habits.

Watch your habits; they become character.

Watch your character; it becomes your destiny."

This will be the benchmark for your change. This saying basically supplies you with the stepping stones of how a belief or habit is formed and the extent to which it can affect your life. The first three lines are going to be your focus for bringing about desired change that will become your destiny.

Your blueprint for lasting change will begin with your thoughts, words and actions. Each leads to improvement of the next, which leads to the lasting change you want. So, let's take a look at some of the steps you can take to begin your journey down the path of everlasting change.

First, you must establish a strong belief that what you are attempting is not merely a possibility, but rather an avouchment to what you are changing. There must be no doubt or wavering in your belief that the change will happen. As you know from experience in life, anything you have attempted that seemed like a difficult undertaking required a firm belief in the outcome. The presence of doubt would only cause you to have missteps along the way. If not controlled, this doubt could become powerful enough to cause you to falter.

Once you have established the belief that you are changing and the new belief that will replace it, you must develop a program or roadmap that will break your task into easier steps. One of the benefits of planning your change in steps is that you can see your progress as you complete each step along the way.

"The moments of happiness we enjoy take us by surprise. It is not that we seize them, but that they seize us." -Ashley Montagu

So let's change the belief that you cannot lose weight and will always be fat. I know saying fat is not politically correct, but it is most likely the word people with this belief use in describing themselves. Now we must break down the steps that we will set for each day. As I said, you want to keep them small and simple so you will be able to see your progress as you go along.

Your first steps might include:

- Setting a regular bedtime so you get the required hours of rest needed. Going to bed at a predetermined time each night is healthy for both your mind and body.
- Set you alarm so you get up 30 minutes earlier than you do now. Take a 15 minute walk to get your mind and body alert for the day ahead.
- Plan your lunch and dinner before you go to work. If you bring lunch to work, have it ready to go the night before.
- Buy yourself some healthy snacks for home and work. You should have them on hand at both places in the event that you get hungry.

- Plan some healthy activities for your day. Keep them simple to start and build on them as you go along.

This is just a few ideas on how you can begin. The point here is to provide yourself with some structure in your daily life. The steps are small to begin with so you can get your mind going in the direction of positive change, as well as see the progress you are making.

Be very specific in your plans for this change. Vagueness will lead to uncertainty which can be the biggest hurdle you can put in your path. Know each and every step and exactly how you will implement them along the way. If you stumble and miss a step be sure to look at it with the mindset of a small error and determine how it happened so you can fix it for the future.

"Happiness is never stopping to think if you are." -Palmer Sondreal

Remind yourself daily of your commitment to this change and what you can expect as you work toward your goal. Start a journal to record your progress and to remind yourself of your total commitment to your goal. If you are a visual person, look at yourself as being 10 or 20 pounds lighter. Do not think in the future, think of now, always in the present moment. Do not visualize what you will look and feel like in the future, experience it now. See yourself as lighter, healthier, and happier now. Look in the mirror and see yourself with the weight gone. See yourself feeling healthier now.

Use avouchment, most people call this affirmations, to bring positive thoughts to yourself every day. Make a recording of these and listen to it whenever you have a chance. Be happy with the plan and your steps to reaching your goal. Be thankful for the progress you are making and smile at yourself for being so dedicated to the end goal.

In this example I have used weight loss, but no matter the change desired you must be unwavering and total. You deserve to live the best life possible. You deserve to live the healthiest life possible. Most importantly, you deserve to live the happiest life possible. It is all within your reach by taking one small step at a time.

The Joy Within

I hope this book has given you a fresher look at the unlimited happiness available to you. It is my goal to provide materials to all those who want to create a better, more satisfying life. If I have been able to help just a few people on their way to a deeper and more satisfying happiness, then I am one happy and successful man.

My life has had its share of sorrowful times. Some of which, at the time they were occurring, tested my resolve to ever having happiness in my life again. I got through these times with the help of family and a very special group of young friends who taught me that life has so much to offer.

Now, it is my life's wish to help anyone I can to find the happiness we all deserve, and to show those going through tough times that they are not alone. I seek to help others better understand the power within each of us to find a happiness they thought only existed in fairy tales.

"How simple it is to see that we can only be happy now, and there will never be a time when it is not now." -Gerald Jampolsky

Please visit my Website for other eBooks on coping with daily life. Feel free to share the FREE eBooks with others. I hope this has helped in some way. I wish you all the happiness you desire; it is yours for the taking.

Sincerely,

James Monty

ThoughtsinPen

www.ingramcontent.com/pod-product-compliance
Lightning Source LLC
Chambersburg PA
CBHW061445040426
42450CB00007B/1218